20 CHART

Including

I GOTTA FEELING
POKERFACE
DON'T STOP BELIEVIN'
& many more...

WISE PUBLICATIONS
PART OF THE MUSIC SALES GROUP

LONDON / NEW YORK / PARIS / SYDNEY / COPENHAGEN / BERLIN / MADRID / HONG KONG / TOKYO

Published by

WISE PUBLICATIONS
14-15 Berners Street, London W1T 3LJ, UK

Exclusive Distributors:

MUSIC SALES LIMITED
Distribution Centre, Newmarket Road,
Bury St Edmunds, Suffolk IP33 3YB, UK

MUSIC SALES PTY LIMITED
20 Resolution Drive,
Caringbah, NSW 2229, Australia

Order No. AM1001044
ISBN 978-1-84938-609-8
This book © Copyright 2010 Wise Publications,
a division of Music Sales Limited.

Edited by Jenni Wheeler.
Cover designed by Lizzie Barrand.

Printed in the EU

www.musicsales.com

YOUR GUARANTEE OF QUALITY
As publishers, we strive to produce every book
to the highest commercial standards.
The music has been freshly engraved and the book has
been carefully designed to minimise awkward page turns
and to make playing from it a real pleasure.
Particular care has been given to specifying acid-free,
neutral-sized paper made from pulps which have not been
elemental chlorine bleached. This pulp is from farmed
sustainable forests and was produced with special regard
for the environment.
Throughout, the printing and binding have been planned
to ensure a sturdy, attractive publication which should
give years of enjoyment.
If your copy fails to meet our high standards,
please inform us and we will gladly replace it.

Bad Boys

Words & Music by Alex James, James Busbee, Larry Summerville,
Lauren Evans & Melvin Watson

1. Some peo - ple call them play - ers but I'm far from
2. Some think it's com - pli - ca - ted, but they're straight up

ter - ri - fied._____ 'Cause some - how I'm drawn to dan - ger
fun for me._____ I don't need no ex - pla - na - tion,

and have been all of my life._____ It feels my
it's noth-ing more than what you see._____ My heart still

heart's div - i - ded half - way 'tween wrong and right._____
feels div - i - ded half - way 'tween wrong and right._____

-dic - ted to them rough - er fel - las. With e - ven the al - pha - bet she on - ly sings the crook - ed let - ters.

Let mam - ma take all the risks for that chem - is - try she like 'em tough - er than leath - er.

Not e - ven a pause, it's more like a ma - ma beat out most dec - i - mal reg - 'lar.

By an - y means ne - ces - sa - ry, girl, she like 'em ruth - less, that's my

Broken Strings

Words & Music by James Morrison, Fraser T. Smith
& Nina Woodford

Original key: Bb minor

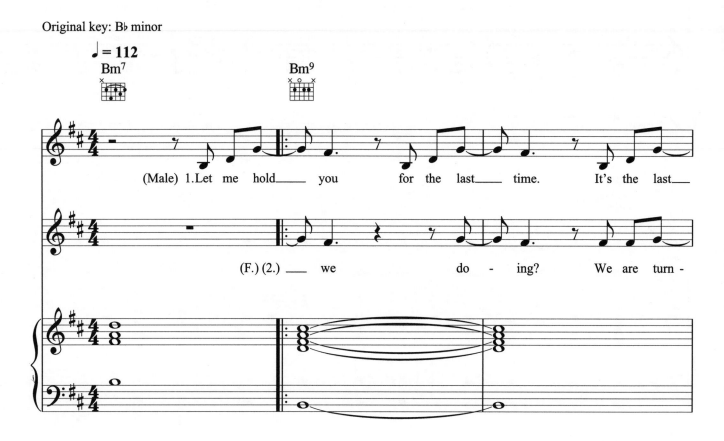

(Male) 1. Let me hold you for the last time. It's the last

(F.) (2.) we do - ing? We are turn -

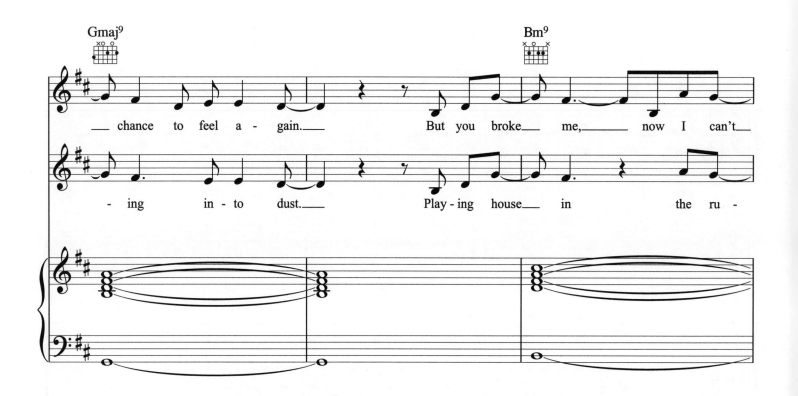

- chance to feel a - gain. But you broke me, now I can't

- ing in - to dust. Play - ing house in the ru -

tears___ me___ up.___ I try to hold on,___ but it hurts___ too much.___ I

try to for - give,___ but it's not___ e - nough to make it all O. K.___ You can't play___

___ on bro - ken strings.___ You can't feel___ an - y - thing___ that your heart___

The Climb

Words & Music by Jessica Alexander & Jon Mabe

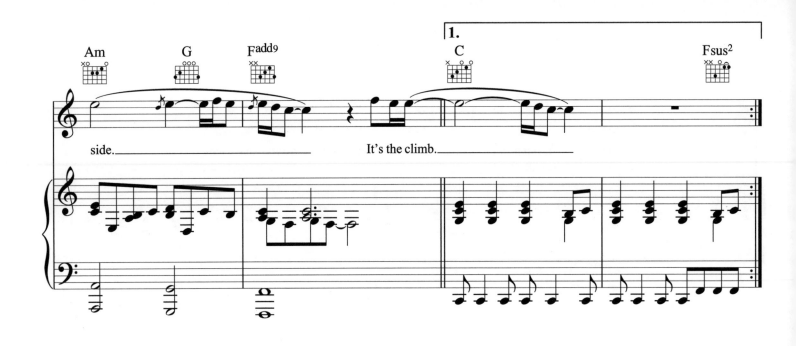

side._____ It's the climb._____

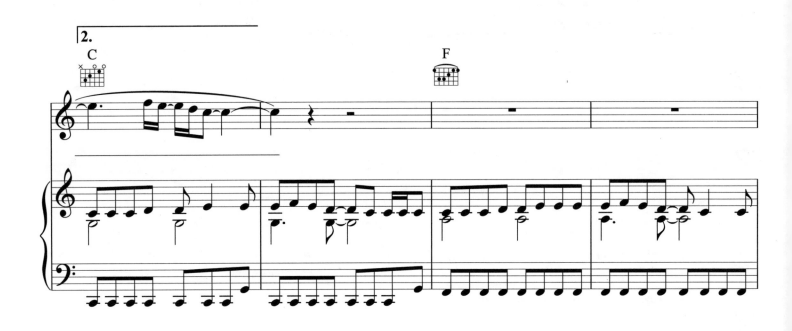

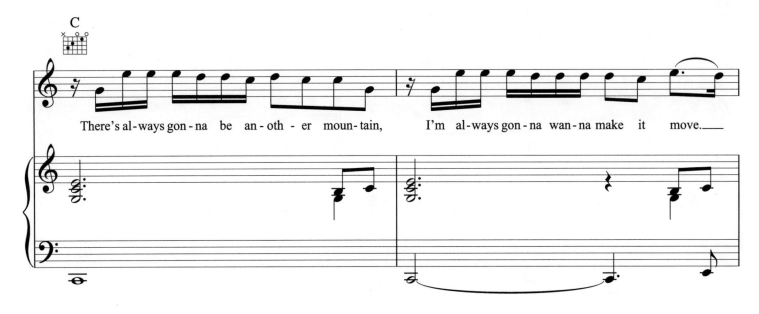

There's al-ways gon-na be an-oth-er moun-tain, I'm al-ways gon-na wan-na make it move.____

(Lead vocal ad lib.)

(There's al-ways gon-na be an-oth-er moun-tain, I'm al-ways gon-na wan-na make it move.___

Al-ways gon-na be an up-hill bat-tle. Some-times I'm gon-na have to lose.___ Ain't a-bout how fast I get there.)

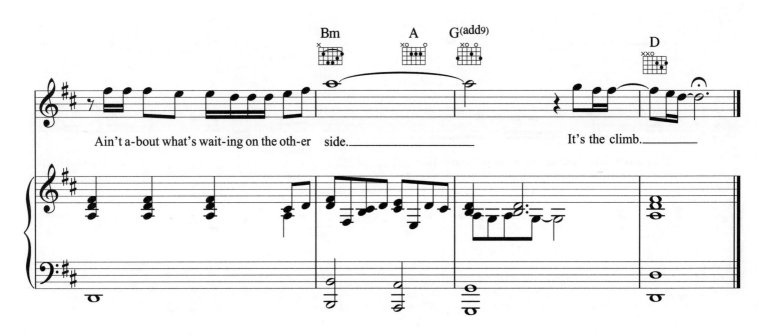

Ain't a-bout what's wait-ing on the oth-er side.___ It's the climb.___

Cry Me Out

Words & Music by Pixie Lott, Mads Hauge, Phil Thornalley
& Colin Campsie

1. I got your e-mails. You just don't get fe-males, now, do___ you?___
2. When I found out how you messed me a-bout I was bro-ken.___

Back

24

Don't Stop Believin'

Words & Music by Steve Perry, Neal Schon & Jonathan Cain

2. A sing-er in a smo-key room,‿ the smell of wine‿ and cheap per-fume.‿

For a smile‿ they can share the night. It goes on and on‿ and on‿ and on.‿

Fireflies

Words & Music by Adam Young

1. You would not be-lieve your eyes if ten__ mil-lion fire - flies
2. 'Cause I'd__ get a thou-sand hugs from ten__ thou-sand light-ning bugs

lit up the world_ as I fell a - sleep.____
as they tried to teach_ me how to dance;____

'Cause they'd fill the o - pen air
a fox__trot a-bove my head,

and leave_ tear-drops ev - 'ry - where. You'd think_ me rude_ but I___ would just stand and
a sock_ hop be - neath my bed,__ a dis - co ball_ that's just__ hang - ing by a

1.

A♭   E♭/G   B♭sus4

stare.
thread.

I'd like to make_ my-self be-lieve____   that pla-net earth____

A♭   E♭   Gm   A♭   E♭

___ turns   slow - ly.   It's hard to say___ that I'd rath - er stay a -

-wake when I'm__ a-sleep. 'Cause ev-'ry-thing is nev-er as__ it seems.__

2.

I'd like to make my-self be-lieve__ that pla-net earth__ turns

slow - ly. It's hard to say__ that I'd rath-er stay a - wake when I'm__ a - sleep. 'Cause

Halo

Words & Music by Ryan Tedder, Beyoncé Knowles & Evan Bogart

46

Fight For This Love

Words & Music by Steve Kipner, Wayne Wilkins
& Andre Merritt

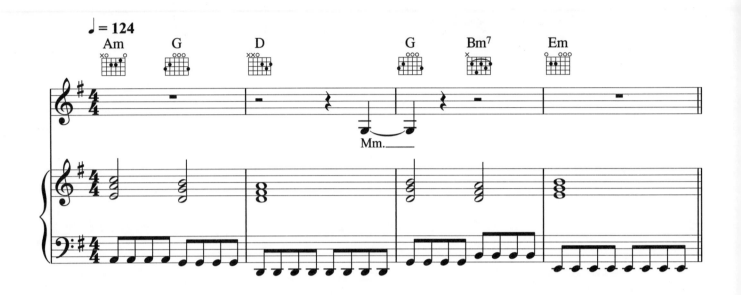

51

I'm Yours

Words & Music by Jason Mraz

more.. It can - not wait. I'm yours._____

Well, o - pen up your mind and see__ like me.__ O - pen up your plans and, damn,__ you're free.

dear,   and I will nib-ble your ear._____   *Scat sing...*

I've been spend-ing

way too long_ check-ing my tongue in the mir - ror and bend-ing o-ver back-wards just to try to see it clear- er.   But

my breath fogged up the glass,_ and so I drew a new face_ and I laughed._____ I

guess what I'll be say - ing is there ain't no bet - ter rea - son to

rid your - self of van - i - ties and just go with the sea - sons. It's

what we aim to do. Our___ name is___ our vir - tue. But

I Gotta Feeling

Words & Music by Will Adams, Jaime Gomez, Allan Pineda,
Stacy Ferguson, David Guetta & Frederic Riesterer

I got-ta feel

just take it   off.   Let's paint the town.   We'll shut it down.

Let's burn the roof   and then we'll do it a - gain._____   Let's do it,   let's

do it,   let's do it, let's do   it,___   and do   it,   and   do it.   Let's live   it up, and

do   it,   and do it,   and   do it, do it, do it.   Let's   do it.   Let's do it.   Let's

71

Little Lion Man

Words & Music by Marcus Mumford

1. Weep

for your- self, my man you'll nev- er be what is in your___ heart.___

Weep, lit - tle li - on man, you're not as brave as you were at the___

___ start.___

Rate your- self and rake your- self,

take all the cou- rage you have___ left.

And

2. Trem-ble for your-self, my man, you know that you have seen this all be - fore._____

did-n't I my dear? Did-n't I my

dear.

Ah.

Ah.

But it was

not your fault, but mine.___ And it was your heart on the line.___ I real-ly

New York

Words & Music by Paloma Faith & Jodi Marr

Original key: G# minor

don't want to hear it. Your new laugh-ter lines, I don't wan-na hear it. The

new-found friends she in-tro-duced you to, I don't wan-na know them I just

wan-na be with you. Please don't make me go to New York,

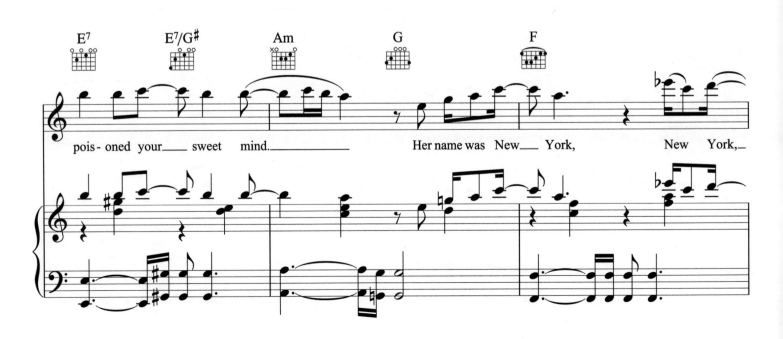

Poker Face

Words & Music by Stefani Germanotta & Nadir Khayat

mah.)1. I wan-na hold 'em like they do in Tex-as, please.
2. I wan-na roll with him, a hot pair we will be.

Fold 'em, let 'em hit me, raise it,
A lit - tle gam - bl - ing is

ba - by stay with me. (I love it.) Luck and in - tu - i - tion play the cards with spades to start, and
fun when you're with me. (I love it.) Rus-sian Rou-lette is not the same with - out a gun; and

af - ter he's been hooked I'll play the one that's on his heart.
ba - by, when it's love, if it's not rough it is - n't fun.

(Oh, whoa,_ oh,

oh, oh,_____ oh.) I'll get him hot, show him what I've got._

N.C.

-po-po-ker face._(Muh, muh, muh, mah.) Po-po-po-po-ker face, po - po-po-ker face._(Muh, muh, muh,

2.

- po-po-ker face._(Muh, muh, muh, mah.) (Muh, muh, muh,

mah.)

(*Spoken*:) *I won't tell you that I love you, kiss or*
(Muh, muh, muh, mah.)

hug you, 'cause I'm bluff- in' with my muf- fin'; I'm not ly- ing, I'm just stun- nin' with my love glue-gunn- in'.

Just like a chick in the ca - si - no, take your bank be - fore I pay you out. I prom - ise this,
(Mah.)

(freely) promise this; check this hand,
'cause I'm marvellous!

G#m

E   E/F#

Can't read my,— can't read my,— no he can't read - a my

B

F#/A#   F#   G#m

po - ker face.—   (She's got me like no - bod - y.)   Can't read my,— can't read my,—

E   E/F#   B   F#/A#   F#

Play 3 times

— no he can't read - a my   po - ker face.—   (She's got me like no - bod - y.)

Many Of Horror
(When We Collide)

Words & Music by Simon Neil

we col-lide, we come to-geth-er. If we don't we'll al-ways be a-

-part. I'll take a bruise, I know you're worth it.

When you hit me, hit me hard.

Sit-ting in a wish-ing hole. Hop-ing it stays dry.

It's you and me till the end of time._____ When we col- lide, we come to-geth- er.

If we don't, we'll al - ways be a - part. I'll

take a bruise, I know you're worth it. When you hit me, hit me hard._____

Sweet Disposition

Words & Music by Lorenzo Sillitto & Abby Mandagi

105

mo - ment,_ a love, a dream, a lie. Just stay_

_ there_____ 'cause I'll_

_ be com - ing o - ver._____

While our blood's_ still young, so_

She Said

Words & Music by Benjamin Ballance-Drew, Eric Appapoulay,
Casell & Tom Goss

Original key: E♭ minor

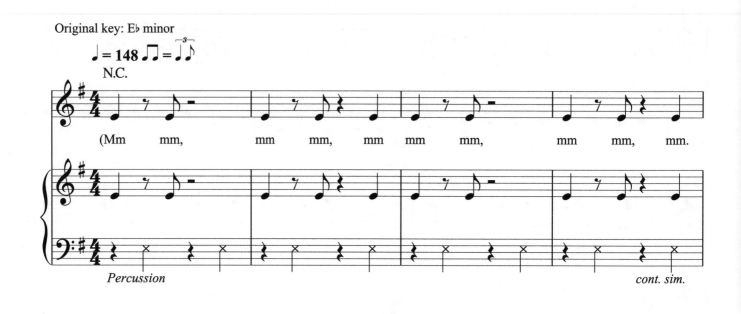

oh, oh, oh, oh,_____ oh."_____

She said "I love you more than words can say."_

She said "I love you ba - a - a - a - a - by."_____

111

So I said___ "What you're say-ing girl, it can't be right.___ How can you be in love with me?___ We on-ly just met to-night."___ So she said___

"Boy, I loved you from the start.___

When I first heard_ 'Love Goes Down'_ some-thing start-ed burn-ing

in my heart."___ I said "Stop___ this cra - zy

talk,_____ and leave right

113

1.

She just feels re - ject - ed, had her heart bro-ken by some-one she's ob-sessed with.
This has got big-ger than I ev - er could have planned,

2.

G

like that song by the Zu - tons, 'Val - er - ie'. 'Cept the jur - y don't look like they're buy-ing it,

B

this is mak - ing me ner - vous. Arms crossed, screwed face, like I'm try-ing it,

G

their eyes fixed on me like I'm mur-der-ous. They wan - na lock me up

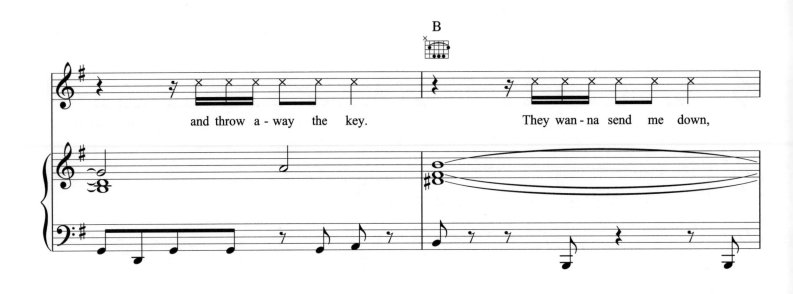

and throw a-way the key. They wan-na send me down,

e-ven though I told them she...

Drums

D.S. al Coda II

116

Starry Eyed

Words & Music by Ellie Goulding & Jonny Lattimer

Fm E♭/B♭ D♭/A♭

1. Han - dle bars that I let___ go,___ let go___ for an - y - one.___
2. So we burst in - to col - ours,___ col - ours___ and ca - rou - sels.___

Fm E♭/B♭ D♭/A♭

Take me in and I'll throw___ out___ my___ heart___
Fall head in first like pa - per planes and___ play-

Cm⁷ Fm

___ and get a new___ one.___ }
- ground___ games.___

Next thing, we're touch - ing. You

A♭add9 D♭6

look at me, it's like you hit me___ with light - ning.___ Ah,___ ah.___

Try Sleeping With A Broken Heart

Words & Music by Jeff Bhasker, Alicia Keys & Patrick Reynolds

And e-ven at the bot-tom of the sea, I could still hear in - side— my

head, tell - in' me, touch me, feel— me._____

And all the time you were tell - in' me lies._____ So, to-night_

I'm gon-na find a— way to make— it with - out— you. To-night_

Gm Csus⁴ C F Gm⁷ F/A B♭ F/A

I'm gon-na find a___ way to make___ it___ with-out you.___

Gm Csus⁴ C F Gm⁷ F/A B♭ F/A

I'm gon-na hold___ on___ to the times___ that___ we___ had, to -

Gm Csus⁴ C F Gm⁷ F/A B♭ *To Coda* ⊕

-night,___ I'm gon-na find___ a___ way to make___ it with-out___ you.

B♭ C F B♭

2. Have you ev - er tried sleep-in' with a bro-ken heart?___ Well, you could try sleep - in' in___ my

bed,   lone - ly,   own me,   no - bod - y ev - er shut it down___ like___

you.   You wore the crown,___   you made my bod - y feel heav - en bound.___   Why don't you

hold me,   need me,   I thought you told me   you'd nev - er leave___ me?___

___ 3. Look - in' in the sky   I could see your face,___   and I know right where I___ fit

in. Take me, make me, you know that al - ways be in
D.S. al Coda
Csus4
F Gm7 F/A B♭
3fr
F/A
love with you, right till the end. Oh, so to-night
Coda
Dm7/G
An - y - bod - y could have told you right from the start,
F/A
B♭
it's 'bout to fall a - part. So rath - er than hold on to a bro - ken dream,

131

Use Somebody

Words & Music by Caleb Followill, Nathan Followill,
Jared Followill & Matthew Followill

let it out. Go let it out. Go let it out. Go

let it out. Go let it out. Go let it out.

Some-one like you.

Whatcha Say

Words & Music by Imogen Heap, Jonathan Rotem,
Kisean Anderson & Jason Derülo

Original key: B major

♩ = 75

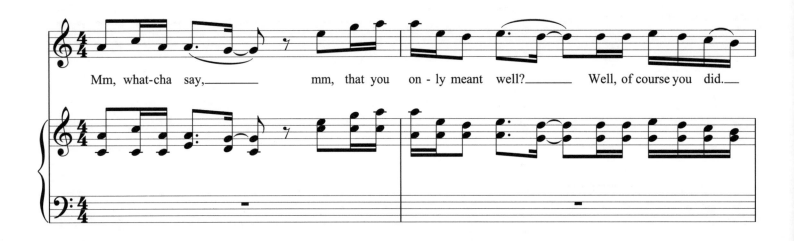

1. I was so wrong for so long On - ly try-'na please my - self._ (My - self.)_ Girl,
2. How could I live with my - self know-ing that I let our love go?_ (Love go.)_ And

I was caught up in her lust when I don't real-ly want no-one else._ So,_
ooh, what'd I do with one chance._ I just got-ta let_ you know._

no, I know I should-'ve treat-ed you bet - ter,_ but me and you were meant to last for - ev - er._
I know_ what I did was-n't clev - er,_ but me and you were meant to be to - geth - er._

So let me in,_ give me an-oth-er chance_ to real-ly be your_ man._
So let me in, give me an-oth-er chance_ to real-ly be your_ man._ } 'Cause when the

Bringing you the words and the music

All the latest music in print... rock & pop plus jazz, blues, country, classical and the best in West End show scores.

- Books to match your favourite CDs.

- Book-and-CD titles with high quality backing tracks for you to play along to. Now you can play guitar or piano with your favourite artist... or simply sing along!

- Audition songbooks with CD backing tracks for both male and female singers for all those with stars in their eyes.

- Can't read music? No problem, you can still play all the hits with our wide range of chord songbooks.

- Check out our range of instrumental tutorial titles, taking you from novice to expert in no time at all!

- Musical show scores include *The Phantom Of The Opera*, *Les Misérables*, *Mamma Mia* and many more hit productions.

- DVD master classes featuring the techniques of top artists.